A HISTORY OF THE CETACEAN AMERICAN DIASPORA

ALSO BY JENNA LE
Six Rivers

A HISTORY OF
The Cetacean American Diaspora

⋅(POEMS)⋅

Jenna Le

© 2018 Jenna Le

Author photo: Minhha Nguyen

Cover photo: Musicman80

Cover and book design: adam b. bohannon

Book editor: Michael Broder

Published by Indolent Books,

an imprint of Indolent Arts Foundation, Inc.

www.indolentbooks.com

Brooklyn, New York

ISBN-13: 978-1-945023-19-4

CONTENTS

I. *And God created great whales*
    A History of the Cetacean American Diaspora   3
    Suckling   4
    Nursery Rhyme   5
    Mirror Gazing   6
    Gather Ye Close-Ups While Ye May   7
    Nature Show   8
    Fishing   10
    Whale Song   11
    Majorca, May 1936   13
    Death Anniversary   16
    The First Time I Saw the Sea   17
    Transmigration   18
    The Nymph's Reply to the Shepherd   19
    Body Dysmorphia   20
    Exodus   23

II. *And every living creature that moveth*
    Minnesota   29
    Ancestress   30
    Công Binh   31
    Why My Friend Heng Lives in Thailand   33
    Birthmark   34

Folk Tale   35
The Faerie Queen Speaks   36
Mitsu   37
Father and Son   40
Chè Bắp   41
Bánh Xu Xê   43
Phrasebook   44
Sonnet Written on the Way Home
from the Cinema   45
My Imaginary Life as a Narcoleptic   46
Baba Yaga   48
Prom Night   51
Tracks   52
Punch Clock   53
A Radiologist's Ghazal   54
A Bruxist Manifesto   55
Almost Abecedarian   57
Nightmare   58
The Patient   60

III. *And every winged fowl after his kind*
Tidal Breathing   65
Our Metaphors Don't Describe Us; They *Are* Us   67
On Being Asian American   68
Embryology and Art   70
Psych!   71
Birth Control   72
This is how you subjugate the Muse   74
Book Report   76
Ark   78

Acknowledgements   81
About the Author   83
About Indolent Books   83

1.

And God
created
great whales

A History of the Cetacean American Diaspora

Zoologists inform us that the whale
evolved from a four-legged grassland mammal,
a pampas-dwelling grampus, a rope-tailed
veldt-roamer. This slope-nosed primeval camel

some million years ago made up his mind
to settle in new digs beneath the sea,
exchanging hooves for flippers, sky for brine.
—The whale's a child of immigrants, like me.

I know the burn the surf-drunk humpback feels
when, self-flung, he up-flounces out of water,
dashing the sun's hot sclera with salt splatter.

I also know the glacial chill that seals
his tug-sized heart off from the universe
when, flubbing flight, he drops back down with force.

Suckling

The milk produced by humpback whales is pink.
The calf rolls over on his side, his inky
lips glued to his mother's tit, and drinks
thick cream the color of diluted blood.

I've long forgot the taste of the milk wrung
from my mother's breasts in infancy. I've tongued
her blood in drugged dreams only. Once, when young,
I punched her bicep, but it didn't bleed.

Despite our differences, we'd go in summer,
she and I, to the fairgrounds by the river
where vendors hawked fried alligator liver,
hand-dyed batiks, beers, Himalayan bloodstones.

I'd stand there, shaded by a red striped tent,
a foaming cup clutched in my prepubescent
hands. They sold it for one dollar ninety cents:
strawberry milk. Its coldness soothed my blood.

Nursery Rhyme

Jonah was a little worm,
a virulent, black-spit-filled germ
that took up lodgings in the churning,
aching abdomen of the whale.

His callused, chitinous finger-nubs
scratched and scraped and drummed and drubbed
the puffy swollen membranes of
the aching abdomen of the whale.

Did he come to filch the ambergris?
Or to see the sights of the abyss,
the blubber-buttered, krill-encrusted,
rubbery rectum of the whale?

What jerk would go spelunking here?
Of all the caves that dimple the sphere,
what idiot would commandeer
my aching abdomen? groaned the whale.

Mirror Gazing

Your belly is a whale
a puffy blue whale
skin lined with downy hairs

Your navel is the whale's eye
a sluggish pupil
clapped between two fatty eyelids

Your vulva is the whale's beak
its heavy ice-cold lips

Your blowhole, at times,
emits faint vapors of ambergris

Gather Ye Close-Ups While Ye May

O how I joy in being photographed,
my chin thrust forward like a strong-jawed fish
so that my neck looks elongate, my lips
daubed red and waxy, each cheek a raft
weighed down with pink cosmetic powder, soft
as earth-warmed snow. When that lens, an ellipse
of glass no bigger than a thumbnail, nips
me from across the room, my eyes go daft,
unfocused: mushy crayon stubs. I gaze
and gaze at portraits of myself with bliss
and adoration, self-love and self-praise.

Ten years from now, it will not be like this.
Ten years from now, the fish's skin will turn crisp
in a copper pan above a kitchen blaze.

Nature Show

Stomach to stomach, face to face,
aquatic mammals couple. Two
bared underbellies, white as glue,
come close, then touch in just one place:

the baldest place. Two narrow snouts
knife past each other in the dark.
We see it all. The misty arc
of each one's joy-clinched form. The spout

of microbe-muddied seawater
that helps perpetuate the pod.
Her muscled tail fin is too broad
for him to mount her like a cur,

and so these dolphins have no choice
but to assume a face-to-face
position, freckled footballs poised
against each other in deep space

where gravity has no import
and where it makes no sense to ask
which one's on top. Whale with two backs,
there is a symmetry in their sport.

There's more than symmetry; there's grace.
Divine, I mean. A chosen few
species meet eyes when they embrace:
bonobos; shrimp; some humans, too.

Fishing

Bearded men who love to fish,
who measure trout by feet and inches;
stout men who read Percy Bysshe
in dories that the daylight drenches
and who hum a little while they wait
for a walleye's jaws to seize their bait....
These men seem grand as Gilgamesh
to me; they are what you'd call *mensches*.

I wish them health and happiness;
I wish them long-lived marriages.
It pains me more than you can guess
to hear that So-and-So and his
bohemian wife, a young *artiste*
with a pixie haircut and slim waist,
have filed for divorce (she left
because "the champagne had lost its fizz").

If men as grand as Gilgamesh
can't keep their marriages intact,
what hope is there for not-so-special
beasts like us? We wander cracked
and crooked sidewalks, seeking sex,
seeking love or what comes next.
"Bone of my bones, flesh of my flesh":
each day, the words seem more abstract.

Whale Song

for Win Ng

Whales: hunted for eons
by pale-skinned Icelanders,
stern-browed Japanese

Whales: caged like parrots,
taught to dance
by fog-haired women in teal wetsuits

Big chins like bulldogs,
long memories like gods,
huge dicks like barnyard ducks

Like lovers,
they eat without chewing,
hunt without stirring

Like humans,
they have sex face-to-face,
pausing only to breathe

Sometimes they have group sex.
Were they human, our churches
would revile them

Sometimes, like gods,
whales live among us in our towns,
wearing human masks

Case in point: Win Ng,
an artist born in San Francisco's
Chinatown

Churches
reviled him. But he sang night
and day, like a whale

And so the whales
he painted on mugs
will always sport grins

Majorca, May 1936

> "Make yourself a prostitute for me as I did for you."
> MARGOT RUDDOCK, Yeats's last mistress

You heard Margot sing out your name: "Bill,
come join me in the garden,
I have something I want to show you."
There was an off-kilter quality
to her voice, like a tuning fork whose tines have bent askew,
but you ignored it. You sat down
beside her in the honeysuckle arbor.

That night, you lay wide-eyed under the blanket,
her kisses still viscous on your lips. Couldn't sleep.
Took a book down from the shelf
but couldn't parse the garbled prose.

How urgently you lusted for her saucer-wild eyes,
her fig-plump flesh. You turned seventy last June,
but this canine hankering
proves the life-force in your loins isn't dead.

*

This is how it plays out:

Like a sleepwalker, you totter
to the shimmering arbor where she sits, shoulders hunched,
unspooling lunatic phrases on diary pages.

She invites you to read what she's written,
but it doesn't interest you the way she does.
All you want is to nuzzle her neck like a herd beast,

but, like morning glory,
blue and dangerous,
she cinches her tendrils around your brain.

*

This is how it plays out:

Jumped out a window,
shattered her kneecap,
escaped from the hospital,
stowed away in a boat.
Was apprehended,
straitjacketed,
and locked in a villa
from whose thick oak doors
a nurse in a white cap
wafted every midnight.
Died, frustrated,
her epic poem not yet written.

*

Margot, the day you rocketed into the hereafter,
everyone covered their eyes.
Because you were a disbeliever,
snow powdered your lonely funeral.

But no flames could consume
your grass heart,
no soil could smother your bones.
You pirouetted out of the universe

gracefully, maintaining
that it was not the state
of being dead that you hated
but the state of lying still.

Death Anniversary

After your suicide by drowning,
the whales refrained from beaching
on this coast for one thousand mornings.
But some scores cannot be evened.

The First Time I Saw the Sea

The first boy that I dated weighted down his coif
with so much hair gel that the crest atop his pate
was hard as horses' teeth. But the first man I loved
had curls so soft and yielding, sea-wind seemed to sit
nestled at all times in their depths.

I asked him, once, to drive me to a beach. I hoped
to see hot conch-strewn sand unfurl before my vision
like a bronze sarong warmed by the body it once draped.
But the beach he drove me to was stone-gray and snow-
    ribboned,
its seashells sparse and small as grapes.

Transmigration

In our first afterlife, we'll rut like buffalo.
One day, while we crouch, feral as raccoons,
rumps furred by goldenrod at hot high noon,
a hunter in a coonskin cap will up and go
out the door of his little lop-eared bungalow
and impregnate us with buckshot, till we swoon.
In our second afterlife, we'll be baboons,
huddled on a hilltop where no hunters go;
we'll bite each other's ears and screech with laughter
until at last we're snuffed out by old age.
Finally, in the third life that comes after,
we shall be alligators, tessera-covered,
wrestling with barrel-chested men on stage
by day; by night, we'll wrestle with each other.

The Nymph's Reply to the Shepherd

Date you again? I'd rather kiss a cuttlefish, my sweet!
A cuttlefish has eight long arms; you're cursed with two left
    feet.
You stick to Brooklyn; cuttles swim the open sea all night.
When nervous, cuttles squirt black ink; your ink is pearly
    white.

Body Dysmorphia

As a child I was obsessed with removing
all the hair from my body. My arms, my legs.
If I could make myself smooth as a key,
I reasoned,
I could pass through locked doors.

Raspberries—those hairy gregarious
puckered pink fruits—
disgusted me.

Now, years later, my thyroid gland
has grown hard and cold
as green jade. My belly and buttocks
doughier.

I swim through my daily routines
like a whale:
murk-eyed, risk-averse, filter-feeding.

Shrimp decked in crystal exoskeletons
pile up like mahjongg tiles
in the backstage parts of me,
behind the velvet of my uvula
and the tiled proscenium of my mouth.

The routines are unbroken, yet something
has changed. Something
has contaminated
my sonar signal. Sex,
once tantalizing,
many-armed like the giant squid,
now matters little.

I don't see as well as I once did.
Did I ever see clearly?
Some writers' eyes
are like camera lenses,
not missing a single
visible detail.

Mine have always been more
like basketball hoops,
stupid, passive, blind.
Only one in a hundred throws
hits the mark,
but the ones that do
make my whole apparatus
shiver like a drum
the drumsticks' blows
have hurt.

And once the vibrations
have stopped,
I find myself standing
in a landscape
I do not recognize.

On a hillside's hard-packed red soil,
mown yellow stubble. Fence posts
with no fence. Flagpoles
with no flag. Rainwater
trickles across the earth's
stony shoulders,
her protuberant moon-bleached
scapulae;
it pools in ditches
and is not absorbed;
the earth has enough
battle-lopped
detritus to digest already.

Exodus

1. THE ROMANTIC VERSION

Dad bellows: *Quick! The spaceship's pulling away
from the dock! Now—jump aboard before the hatch
shuts!* Mom, invariably the calm one, snaps:
*Have you gone nuts? To jump that far would break
our bones!* The harbor teems with tubby gray
bodies of Martians anxious to decamp
from a planet overswept by poison gas.
I put my hand on Sister's mouth, so blazing
vapors can't seep inside her lungs. Dad pays
a hard-eyed rocket crewman 80 gnods
to let the seven of us stow away
within his cargo hold. For sixteen nauts,
we sleep and shit and piss in that small area.
Dad says we'll live like kings once we reach Terra.

2. THE REALISTIC VERSION

Sixth day at sea. The stowaways discover
they outnumber the crewmen, two to one.
"Let's throw those fuckers overboard! How come
they get to sleep on berths with goose-down covers
while we sleep shivering in the hold like dogs?"
one youth croaks. Several others cheer his words.
Dad doesn't want to share a space with murderous
conspirators like these, but knows they'll toss
him to the whales as well if he speaks out

against them. Mom, eyes shut, bemoans her gout.
Sister clings to my concave belly, nestles.
On the eighth day, a U.S. Navy vessel
parts the fog. Law and order are restored.
We're fed milk, apples. I vomit on the floor.

3. THE MODERNIST VERSION
It's June a brown-skinned family of seven
has come to stay in our guest cottage Pop
says space will be tight for a while but God
smiles on the charitable from His heaven
and anyway this is an opportunity
for us to educate these foreign pagans
about the one true faith of Christianity
Mom volunteers to show them how we shop
for groceries here in the U.S.A.
you know small things like that the youngest daughter
and I become fast friends *How do you say
dishwashing where you're from?* I ask one day
and she replies *Rua chen* that night when Pop
says *Sal wash up* I scream *Rua chen sucks cocks*

4. THE POSTMODERNIST VERSION
This is a story with no characters,
just things. A louse plucked, twitching, from a fistful
of hair. A cardboard shrine for the lost. The whir
of a dented record player spinning wistful
tunes like Francoise Hardy's "Ce Petit Coeur"
and Sylvie Vartan's "Quand Le Film Est Triste,"
songs so well-known a listener's eyes would mist
to hear them, if there were a listener.
But this stern story has no characters,

just places. The bodega in New York
at which he purchased his first cigarettes.
The waterfall in Albuquerque where
she got her blouse with the neck ruffle wet.
The heartland town where they now live and work.

II.

*And every
living creature
that moveth*

Minnesota

Here, the sly West Wind waylaid sweet Wenonah.
This same breeze, some centuries before,
blew headstrong Helen's skiff toward Troy's wine kraters.
One and the same gust, some lifetimes later,
pushed my parents' ship toward U.S. shores.

West Wind, I need you now. Here, no one shores
me up; I have no teacher, no translator,
no one to stop me from stumbling into craters.
Panther-straddling god of poems, I am for
you and only you. Kiss me like you kissed Wenonah.

Ancestress

This lady was so devout,
her hair remained
lush and black as
squirted squid ink
until age eighty-three,

and when her spinster
daughter came to tidy
after the funeral,
recalling her mother's
wrinkled snail-face,

she half-expected
to see a sloughed cobra skin
curled on the bed she died in.
But no: not even
a smudge of sweat.

Công Binh

Boss knew I had a name, but never used it. Couldn't
   pronounce it.
Didn't care how many aunts I have, or on what beach our
   town sits.
He handed me a printed card to hold and took my mugshot.
The card read: Z A O 1 6. The ship's hold smelled like dogshit,

and it was dark. The man beside me had sharp bony
   shoulders
and sniffed all night. The voyage lasted weeks. Marseille was
   colder
than I expected, and I shivered in the clothing given.
Boss gestured at some tents, said: "This is where you boys'll
   be living."

Barbed wire ran round the tents. Cars took us to and from
   the factory
each dawn and dusk. We toiled till we were sick. One man
   got bacteremia
and died in the infirmary. Another was blown to atoms
when powder he'd been told to mix caught fire: white smoke
   enwrapped him.

One day, the French boss disappeared; a German boss took
   over.

"You Indochinese dogs will answer to me now," he blustered. Things went on like this till the June of 1944.

We asked no questions, toiled on. It was war, but not our war.

Why My Friend Heng Lives in Thailand

My childhood friend, Heng, trained a cock with wart-hard
feet for cockfights. It lived out in the courtyard,
bossing the hens his parents raised for eggs.
Heng would tenderly stroke its scabrous legs
for hours. Once, I saw him rip up bits
of savory pigskin, chew them soft, then spit
them in the rooster's open maw. Like a mother.

What he loved, he loved deeply. The one other
soul he doted on as much as that bird
was a stoop-backed monk whom he'd encountered
volunteering at pagoda: kindly, ill, old.
He kept that old man's photo in his billfold.

His dad, a jealous sort, so envied this love
that, in a rage, he strangled the chicken... What then?
Well, then Heng met the Bangkok beauty. Moved.
Never spoke to his family again.

Birthmark

Born with a birthmark splotched on her right cheek
and none on her left, she harbored in her lopsided
noggin since toddlerhood the barmy thought
that asymmetry was what made the world tick.

When things were viewed this way, they all made sense:
the fact that one of her parents was tall, one stout;
the fact that Mother chirped all day, while frowny
Dad just grunted—"Yes... No... That's what I *meant*";

the fact that her big brother always got
the gooier slice of cake, the heirloom watch,
the coo of praise. *All things in life, even love,*

are skew, mon chou! the cosmos seemed to taunt.
A lady, she always dated two men at once:
one she fawned on, one she kept in reserve.

Folk Tale

My mother tells a folk tale from Vietnam:
a woman's husband goes off to soldier
and leaves behind a son who does not know him.
One night, the woman holds up in the air
a soldier's clothes and, pointing to their shadow,
tells her lonely child, "That is your dad."
Years pass. The vet comes home. The boy cries, "Dad?
You're not my dad! My dad is black, like shadow."

The tale concludes the way you might expect:
the woman slain, her husband locked away
in prison. He's contrite, but it's too late.
Like Shakespeare's Moor, his war-frayed mind was pecked
to pieces by misguided jealousy.
Like peace, our pity for him comes years late.

The Faerie Queen Speaks

Come kiss me, you scarfaced old-timer.
Come embrace me, my postpubescent pet.

Unwind my hundred-year-old obi. Strip off my mod designer
  threads, my green hand-woven kirtle, my Hello Kitty™
  barrette.

Let me show you Faerieland. Relax. Lie back on my recliner.
I'm the toast of the town in Ed Koch's Manhattan and 8 B.C.
  Tibet.

What's your name again? Thomas the Rhymer?
Urashima the Fisherman? How fast an old dame like me
  forgets.

Mitsu

At my first job, an office assistant
named Mitsu, a woman draped
loosely in dowdy clothes always
brushing the cotton shoulders
of her drab blouse, worked:
I later learned
she had a son in college,
so she must've been middle-aged,
but her face was enamel-
smooth, its appearance of apricot-
glossy youth well-preserved,
so I treated her informally,
with the casual city manners
I saved for folks my own age. Mitsu
had come down in the world,
gossips murmured: in the country
she immigrated from,
she had sat like a well-fluffed chicken
on a nest of wealth
and family prestige, which all got lost
some years ago, after which she wed
a fat rich American
and moved to Boston. Very lucky for her
it worked out that way,
people said. Mitsu spoke
English imperfectly, so I,

who had been born in the U.S.
and spoke English with no flaw,
viewed her with a speck
of condescension in my eye. Within months
of meeting Mitsu, I began to spin
elaborate fantasies
about her in my mind: I pictured
how I would one day be her savior,
I pictured her
being reduced to tears
by a haughty client, an elderly racist
who'd berate her for her foreign
speech and dress, and I pictured
myself sweeping onto the scene, so puffed
with righteous rage
that without fear of consequences
I'd vocally defend
the wailing Mitsu, demand the racist
apologize to her forthwith,
then hug her and console her while she cried.
Each time I saw Mitsu at work, my brain
added new elements
to this heroic daydream
until it was vivid
as something that really happened.
And then one morning, I showed up at the office
and Mitsu wasn't there:
the secretary told me
in a chummy confidential whisper
that, due to some careless act I had committed

and for which Mitsu had been blamed,
the boss had yelled at Mitsu
and she had left the premises
last night softly weeping.

Father and Son

My son says he don't
wanna become an automotive
man and work the car lot with me,
oh no he's an emotive
washcloth, drenched with
sensitive notions. He intends to
spend these four years dabbling
in word-doodles wearing a goatee and
become a what-you-call-poet. I say
boy when did you ever
see me walk up and down town
catching folks by surprise like
the Cash Cab, gabbing about
what pretty scenes I've been dreaming
in the wee hours, grenades and parades
and naked babes with rabbit ears making
googly eyes at me? Has a man ever lived
who earned respect that way, wattle
quivering with intensity
like an opera queen's? How d'you figure
I got your mom to knuckle under,
by scribbling sonnets or by showing her
the cudgel I lessoned So-and-So with? Passion,
Junior, never skinned any potatoes.

Chè Bắp

In the backyard, Father grew
ears of sweet corn,
green-swaddled blimps
of ocher bluster.

When the wind gusted over,
the stalks bowed so low
their rigid plumes
would graze the cakey dirt.

On the designated day,
Father would gather the ears
and heap them, firewood-like,
in the house;

then Mother, with her
preternaturally clean hands, nearly
too pale to be Vietnamese,
would husk them,

exposing their firmly pebbled
yellow nudity
to her black eyes' scrutiny.
With the only knife in the drawer

precise enough to suit her,
she sliced the cobs
into cylinders
of uniform size—lop! lop!—

then, unclosing her palms,
dropped them to their fate
at the bubbly base
of her simmering black pot.

The corn pudding thus made was called
chè bắp. This was served
in tiny fingerbowls
of swan-white porcelain

that never saw daylight
on any occasion but this.
On the side of each bowl
was tattooed in red

a Chinese motif, meaning "joy."
Five times did I have the pleasure
of tasting *chè bắp*,
of using my spoon to scrape the delicate

skin off the top. Then a scourge of squirrels
wiped out Father's crop.
He and Mother shrugged.
Never again.

Bánh Xu Xê

> "Bánh xu xê *is a traditional cake that is normally served at Vietnamese weddings. The stickiness of the cake symbolizes the stickiness of the marriage ties. The golden filling embodies the loyalty & faithfulness of husband & wife, like a golden heart.*"
> FROM danangcuisine.com

Pandanus amaryllifolius'
svelte leaves, massed like so many shadow puppets,
mob the hut where the newlyweds make love.

The plants that swarm the portholes have a scrubbed
smell, like a grove no dog's yet grimed with droppings.
Pandanus amaryllifolius—

green fans whose roots, like water spiders, pussyfoot
in plain sight—send cockroaches galloping
from the hut where the newlyweds make love.

Like eunuchs wielding chlorophyll katanas,
the plants stand guard while the twined pair lies sleeping.
Pandanus amaryllifolius:

when morning comes, the bride will stand, hair mussed,
in her new kitchen, floury fingers plumping
sweet cakes that symbolize sweet bonded love.

No pastries she makes henceforth on that stove
will taste good as those cakes, those first flawed couplings
when *pandanus amaryllifolius*
blessed the hut where the newlyweds made love.

Phrasebook

The word for "persimmon" is HỒNG,
which also denotes "pink,"
as in a blush, a plethora
of blood that floods the skin.

The word for "mango" is XOÀI,
a string that, coyly, begins
with X and O, like the kisses
and hugs at a letter's end.

He pares the fruits at the sink
with an outsize cleaver, whose sharp
blade detaches tissue-thin
red rind from globous pulp,

moist as a living body,
then feeds me one taut wedge
of watered silk. Not far
from my hot tongue, the knife's edge.

Sonnet Written on the Way Home from the Cinema

Call it reverse racism if you like,
but it enrages me to have to watch
a man of steadfast will and forceful thought—

a man like the Hmong guy selling pike
along the turnpike, or the Thai guy carving
knickknacks for tourists in a roadside booth,

or my own dad, who, in his distant youth,
hawked loaves of bread, shamefaced, to keep from starving—

it angers me to see this kind of fellow
objectified, aestheticized, squashed flat,
diminished to a voiceless scrap of yellow

at the edge of an Anglo moviemaker's shot,
reduced to mute decor at the margins of
a white-skinned artist's film.—*Or call it love.*

My Imaginary Life as a Narcoleptic

When I was seven, I aspired to write
a romance film whose heroine has narcolepsy.
I'd seen on *Dateline NBC* one night,
the TV screen as shimmering and dark as Pepsi,
a piece concerning neurologic oddities:
a man who hoarded trash; a woman who,
surrounded by bacteria, felt not at ease
(she washed her hands exactly forty-two
times daily, to forestall flesh-eating germs);
and, most intriguing, a fat single guy
who, whenever strong emotions squirmed
inside him, fell to snoring instantly.

Though my sleep patterns were normal at age seven,
some prescient corner of my childish mind
made me identify with that unshaven
dough-faced sufferer whose eyes were lined
with purple rings. In my imagination,
I cooked up a romantic tale where I,
a twenty-something narcolepsy patient
with movie-actress cheekbones, nearly die
when slumber overtakes me as I cross
a busy street. A handsome man named John
comes out of nowhere, saves my life. He bossily
growls, "I'll be taking care of you from now on."

John and I move in together. He
teaches me how to manage my condition,
my narcolepsy, and for a time it seems
our love will last forever. Our ambition
exceeds our grasp, though. One chill evening,
I say to John, "I hate to say this, but
I'm leaving you for another man." "I'll wring
your skinny neck, you damned ungrateful slut,"
John answers, lunging at me. My knees buckle,
and instantly I fall asleep. It's thus
that narcolepsy keeps us together shackled.
At seven years old, that's what I thought love was.

Baba Yaga

invites me over, but doesn't answer my knock.
I test the door. It's unlocked.

She's peeling green bell peppers
over the kitchen sink,
letting the peels fall
into a silver colander. I blink:

Baba Yaga's kitchen looks exactly like my mother's
in Minnesota. The same
oily yellow wallpaper,
edges peeling like the inflamed

skin around a wound.
The wall calendar with photos of orchids
my mother liked
because, as she often remarked,

"Purple's the royal color."
The date my report card should arrive by mail
circled in red ink,
like a noose. On a dusty table

next to the calendar,
an ice-blue rotary phone

(I'm five years old, listening
to my mother intone

that I must always say "*May* I please inquire
who is calling?", not "*Can* I please,"
while I glower at her
black-silk-curtained knees).

A bundle of newspapers, opened
to the crossword page, answers penned
in the angular handwriting
I adopted at ten

because I wanted to become an architect,
a "feminine" career.
Our family's first microwave,
which mother feared

would give me cancer.
The worn-down linoleum patch
where I had to stand naked,
breast buds goosefleshed,

so that mother could cut my hair.
Baba Yaga keeps peeling peppers, hums.
I wish I could say
this was one of those dreams

where Baba Yaga's face
turned out to be my mother's,
or a wizened version of my own,
or anything other

than just Baba Yaga
looking exactly as leathery and warty and old
as on my book of Russian fairy tales.
That, by gazing at her, I could be made whole.

Prom Night

When I went to my high school prom
with a boy whose name I cannot ferret
from memory's wells, tall-coiffed like a soufflé
and long-chinned like a carrot,

my mom and dad both squatted on
our scouring-pad-like parlor rug,
crouched low and long so that their buttocks grazed
rough pile, and grinned, and hugged

their boxy cameras to their faces,
snapping over fifty shots
of me and Vague-Eyed Red-Faced Boy, red herring
in my life's love plot,

snapped more than fifty frames of that
inconsequential night in May—
my parents, who don't even have one photo
of their wedding day.

Tracks

At yard sales, I gravitated to
the toy train sets, but Mom
was crazy for ceramics.
She never stuck flowers in any
of the china vases
she bought, but displayed
them bone-dry in a lacquered
cabinet we kids
were not allowed to breathe on.
What's the point of a container

that doesn't contain? I wondered,
having not yet discovered poems.
I never even laid eyes
on a real train
till I was grown. As a teen, I waited
at railroad crossings with starry eyes
for those mythic
beasts to make themselves
known, but, until I was old
and alone, they never came.

Punch Clock

At my old job in downtown Flushing,
we had to punch in and out by touching
our index fingers to a screen.
When I tried to do this, the machine
crowed, "SYSTEM ERROR. SYSTEM ERROR."
Each day, I had to phone up Jerry,
the weedy, pale man from IT,
to sweet-talk the time clock for me.

Like a latter-day horse whisperer,
he thumbed the buttons spiritually. "Sure
you washed your hands today, Ms. Le?
If you've oily skin, the sensor can't see
your fingerprints." When I responded
that yes of course I'd washed, he handed
me a towelette with a soppy grin,
saying, "Well, why not wash again?"

And so I scrubbed my hands once more
while he watched me scrub them. No cigar.
The time clock still refused to function.
"Ah well," sighed Jerry with compunction,
"Looks like no matter how you rinse,
it doesn't like your fingerprints.
Hasn't had a glitch since being installed…
Seems you're not human, after all."

A Radiologist's Ghazal

Good dancing-girls wear grass skirts, I was led
to believe. My skirt is made of solid lead.

They stare dully at my skirt, my unflappable skirt,
the old men who are too ill to rise from bed:

once, I heard one wizened Welshman grumble,
"If fashion's come to this, I may as well be dead."

In these subterranean caves, we are all clothed
with sheets of metal; with barium salts, we're fed.

As a child, I looped one end of a rope around my waist
and, with it, towed uphill a snow-caked sled;

now my hips are sore from the weight of...what?
The adult responsibilities that plague my tired head?

I hide behind my skirt, the way that we as kissing teens
hid behind your father's fox-infested shed.

A Bruxist Manifesto

When I'm asleep, I grind my teeth
unconsciously. There is a word
for this trait: *bruxism*. Like *Marxism*
or any other *ism*, bruxism
is serious stuff—a myrtle wreath
beneath which martyrs are interred.

Studies have shown that bruxists often
suffer from psychiatric ailments,
depression and anxiety
being the commonest maladies.
A bruxist's dreams are filled with coffins,
airplane crashes, train derailments.

My boyfriends have all had to find
some way to cope with it. The glum-
eyed Russian beanpole used to seize
my mandible between his thumb
and forefinger; he'd gently squeeze
the bone until the din declined.

As a result of all the rocking,
rubbing, and rasping my teeth abide,
my jaw joint has been worn quite smooth.
And when I open my mouth wide

to eat a hero (treacherous food!),
the ball can slip out of its socket.

This happened to me as I snacked
with a male colleague at a British
café one time in east Virginia.
Though old in years, his mind was kiddish,
crude-edged. I blushed red as a zinnia
when my jaw did its Houdini act—

escaping from its niche and then
refusing to be coaxed back in—
so that my mouth hung open, drooling,
for several seconds made more grueling
by my male colleague's sexed-up grin.
Henceforth, he called me Snake-Jawed Jen.

"Snake Girl," "Dragon Lady": hurtful names
even when the speaker means no ill.
I grit my teeth. The problem is
I grit my teeth too much. In dreams,
my mouth gapes wide, and oranges
are crammed inside against my will.

Almost Abecedarian

A man I once believed I loved
believed he had
contracted HIV from a cad
drunkenness had driven him into the denim-clad
embraces of:
fortunately, we were both mistaken.
Great was his relief—profuse
joy washed over him, from his chartreuse
kid-leather hat down to his fine suede shoes,
leaving him a shaken
mannequin—when he received the grand
news that his test was clean.
Only someone who has seen,
perilously close, death's keen
quartz eyes fix on where he stands
really understands
such shuddering relief, such ice-cold joy.
Those of us who have never been
unfortunate enough to win
(win!) death's attention
experience a similar excess of feeling when
young love, embodied by a suede-shoed boy,
zips through our lives and we're almost destroyed.

Nightmare

When the nurse found
Monique dead in bed,
her hands were swollen
like pincushions.
Her arms were swollen
like sofa bolsters.
Every part of her body
was abnormally puffy
as if she had been dead
for many hours,
and every square inch of her skin
was sheened in sweat
so that she seemed
to be wearing
a halo made of seawater.
The nurse went
to fetch the intern.
Rubbing the sleep
out of his eyes,
the intern went
to fetch an EKG machine
so that,
in accordance with hospital policy,
he could document that Monique
was truly dead.
But Monique's sweatiness

made her skin so slippery
that the electrodes
of the EKG machine
refused to adhere to it.
Error message
after error message
spooled out of the machine's
leering mouth.
After spending hours
unsuccessfully coaxing
the machine to work,
the intern was beginning
to sweat a bit himself.
Using a corner of Monique's
beige bedsheet,
he furiously tried
to wipe her big breasts dry
so that the electrodes
could find purchase and
the EKG machine would work.
At last it did. The intern
let out an uncouth cheer.
He hugged Monique's
rain-drenched corpse in his glee.
By now, the corpse
was completely cold.

The Patient

His surname's Spanish, but his eyes are shaped
like almonds, like my father's. "Filipino,"
he grins, "And you?" "I'm Vietnamese," I answer.
"How do you feel?" I ask. He shifts his nape
on the hospital pillow. "Doc, this chemo
is something else. I've lived five years with cancer,

and this is the first morning that I've felt
too weak to hit the pool and swim ten laps.
Does everybody feel weak after TACE?"
"Some people do," I say. I prod the welt
in his groin with gloved fingers, note his rapid
pulse rate. He says, "You have such a young face,

Doc, you remind me of my baby daughter—
she started med school just this fall." "How proud
you both must be!" I clap my hands. In Asia,
nothing brings greater pleasure to a father
than the ability to boast about
a child who wears a stethoscope and pager,

and, gazing at the gaunt man stretched before me,
I suddenly remember how my dad
teared up when I received my own diploma.
The patient's eyes, his almond eyes, are stormy

now, his voice thick: "Look, Doc, I know it's bad,
this tumor that I have, this hepatoma.

I know that, in the end, it's sure to kill me.
I am not asking to be saved from death.
All I ask is a chance at witnessing
my Beth get her MD...." And though it fills me
with pain to think of the pressure this puts on Beth,
I wish that I could promise everything.

III.

*And every
winged fowl
after his kind*

Tidal Breathing

There is a duck
patrolling the lake shore,
his seed-like eyes
gazing at the water
as it stretches away from us
like a pewter plate
on which the breezes clink like coins.
His gray cottony belly
drags along the shelves of stone.
Beneath the surface gloss
of his brown breastplate,
his puffed-out chest
harbors two separate fistfuls
of cold oxygen.
His lungs are more evolved, more efficient
than our human lungs,
circulating the diamond-bright
northern air
through a network of tiny tubes and valves
without waste
or sentiment.
It is so superior
to the way we mammals breathe:
our noisy ragged sobs,
our shallow tidal exhalations,
the way our soft fleshy noses

drag morsels of blue sky
into the dark zones
that border our red hearts.
How hard his beak seems,
like the warped yellow wood
of an attic piano.
How rock-hard
his green feathered skull.

Our Metaphors Don't Describe Us; They *Are* Us

The penis of a feral duck, intent
to scourge the black-plumed female of his kind
with brutish thrusts that she did not consent
to, has a monstrous corkscrew shape: it winds
its glistening 18-centimeter length
in counterclockwise fashion round its center.
Roughly, the male duck pounds this spiral oddity
into his mate's submerged bedraggled body.

In Kyoto's culture, ducks, called *oshidori*,
are venerated for their gentleness.
In every ancient Japanese folk story,
ducks, male and female, are portrayed as blessed
with human traits: their souls are changeless kernels,
and their pair bonds are said to be eternal.

On Being Asian American

I bought
this rubber duck
at a novelty store:
not yellow

with an orange beak,
but a vibrant
springtime green
with a corona

of cumulus-white
daisy petals
framing its
unblinking face.

As if its body
were a stem.
As if such a thing
were possible.

Fact: nothing on earth
is allowed to be a duck
and a flower
simultaneously.

Me, I'm not even permitted
to be a duck
and a flower
at two separate times!

Embryology and Art

Each human life starts as an embryo
in which the heart sits high, the brain down low.
Pre-birth, the embryo folds like a bed:
that's how your heart ends up beneath your head.

By allowing this, we share complicity
in a crime as foul as Eve's old apple fraud:
the forceful subjugation of the god
of love to mortal reason's tyranny.

Therefore, from birth, we owe a debt to Cupid,
which we pay off by making works of art
inspired by the preening swan who looped
his neck to put his head below his heart.

Psych!

"A god has taken a shine to you," explains the letter.
She's skeptical, but curiosity compels her.
His face is masked. His name, unsaid. At dawn, one feather

curls on her sheets, the only proof that he's been with her.
Brain fogged, she brews some coffee. Pops an Alka-Seltzer.
"A god has taken a shine to you," explains the letter,

which she rereads. It helps her understand no better.
She slams the cooled mug down. *What* happened *last night,*
    Elsa?
His face was masked. His name, unsaid. At dawn, one feather

was all he left, and now you feel beneath the weather...
Who says "take a shine," anyway—some corny geezer?
"A god has taken a shine to you"—like hell! Damn letter!

She calls in sick to work. Across her sick mind flitters
the thought that she should go to church, confront the greaser
who goes by "God." Real name, unsaid. But there's that feather

she woke beside, which now lies warm against her sweater...
The next time he requests her company, she agrees, her
doubt vanished. This time, there's no need for "god," "shine,"
    "letter."
His face is masked. No names. Next dawn, another feather.

Birth Control

Winging south, we met an Inuit fur trader
snowshoeing upcountry. Buoyed
to see a friendly face
in such desolate parts,
we hooted at him
as a form of greeting. He said,
"Messieurs Owls,
I've been meaning
to ask you something.
I've noticed that in years
when lemmings are scarce,
your speckle-breasted hausfraus
lay fewer eggs
than in years when lemmings
trickle across the tundra
in tens of thousands. Guess they don't
want to hatch an owlet
whose fate is to die hungry.
Yet I never
see them fly into town
to beg the warty-lipped doctor there
for the pills and inserts
our women use
to limit the sizes of families. Pray,
what mode
of birth control do they use?"

Honored sir, esteemed colleague
in the rodent business:
all you need
is to see, just one time,
one of your own hatchlings
shrunk by starvation,
his pale face
a sharp-angled mask,
his yellow eyes hard as white man's coins,
stand hunched
over his brother's bony corpse

and then start gnawing.

This is how you subjugate the Muse

First, you cut her hair.
You let the clippings drop in
a bathtub that has never been wet.
When the tub is full,
you undress, shoes last. You lie down in it

and wait for the tub's claw-feet
to spasm, indicating
the strychnine has leached into the marble's
veins. They'll clench and unclench,
maybe try to scurry.
Ignore your quickening heartbeat,
a noise like newspaper being crumpled

in a distant room. Whatever happens,
don't look directly at
the green soap, whose upcurled ends
resemble a leaf's.
The bald god is testing you.
The bald god is testing you.
Stare hard at the backs of your eyelids

till you feel the vibrations
of the soap taking flight like an airplane, and vanishing.
It's time now.
Count aloud to seven,

allotting a century to each syllable.
Then speak the god's name
coquettishly, the way a female owl calls

for her chosen mate
to bring her a freshly killed rat.

Book Report

Blaga Dimitrova was a Bulgarian poet. She was Vice President of Bulgaria in 1992, when I was a third-grade student in a small brick schoolhouse in Midwest America. The schoolhouse was shaped like a bird, mummy-wrapped in snow.

At eight years old, I didn't know where Bulgaria was. I knew where Vietnam was, because my parents lived there until war speckled their world with red and brown like a stampede of giraffes. Last month, a Danish zookeeper shot a giraffe in the head and fed it to a lion, who ate it slowly, just to be polite. Blaga Dimitrova visited Vietnam as a journalist in the sixties, but she didn't meet my parents.

In 1967, Dimitrova and her husband adopted a Vietnamese girl. Dimitrova was forty-five and childless. I was my mother's second daughter. At eight years old, I wanted to be an astronaut. I longed to be a bird, but I was mummy-wrapped in snow.

Like my parents, Dimitrova was an anti-Communist. She believed that politics need not be antithetical to poetry; one of her poems reads: "The sky moves through the swamp / without becoming muddy."

I once watched a documentary about the fall of Saigon. In the movie, a Vietnamese woman burns all her adult daughter's belongings in a bonfire in their back yard. *It's so that the Communists don't find out you're an America sympathizer and kill you*, she explains. The daughter never speaks to her mother again.

Dimitrova's adopted daughter grew up to be a writer. She published a memoir after Dimitrova died, alleging that Dimitrova's husband raped her. What does *betrayal* mean? In the documentary, a Vietnamese woman shakes her fist because her American G.I. friends deserted Saigon without warning and left her there to die. When I turned eighteen, I moved out of my hometown without a backward glance.

Ark

The second night of the hurricane,
the subways were all flooded.
So I took a taxi
home from the hospital.
That was how I met Ali,
intrepid cab driver
who had immigrated
to New York from Bangladesh.
As he drove, Ali
told me stories about
his late wife, Hoa,
a Vietnamese immigrant
who folded shirts
at a clothing boutique
on the Upper West Side.
Her large Catholic family
disapproved of her
marrying Ali, a Muslim.
But one Sunday, as she knelt in church,
she heard God's voice
tug at her golden earlobe
whispering,
Be fruitful…no, be loving
and marry this man.
Be his wife until you die.
Ali's taxi is watertight,

and it carries him and me,
one male and one female
of the human species,
for many miles through the storm.
I wonder:
how many of those handpicked couples
on Noah's ark really loved each other?
And I remember how
Ali's eyes widened
when, scarcely two feet
ahead of the windshield,
a dove was shaken out of the sky,
the way a woman shakes the knots
out of a long silk scarf.

ACKNOWLEDGEMENTS

Versions of some of these poems were previously published by the following journals, sometimes under other titles:

AGNI Online: "A Radiologist's Ghazal" (2012)
Amarillo Bay: "Ancestress" (2014)
American Arts Quarterly: "Prom Night" (2016)
Asian American Literary Review: "Body Dysmorphia," "Phrasebook" (2015)
Bellevue Literary Review: "Almost Abecedarian" (2013)
Cha, an Asian Literary Journal: "Ark" (2014)
Chattahoochee Review: "Binh Explains Why His Brother Lives in Spain" (2015)
Crab Creek Review: "On Being Asian American" (2012)
Crab Orchard Review: "Sonnet Written on the Way Home From the Cinema" (2015)
Dislocate: "This Is How You Subjugate the Muse" (2014)
Echolocation: "Nursery Rhyme" (2014)
Epiphany: "*Bánh Xu Xê*" (2014)
Hayden's Ferry Review: "Book Report" (2014)
Houseboat: "Fishing" (2014)
Hyphen Magazine: "Birth Control" (2015)
Innisfree Poetry Journal: "Birthmark," "Punch Clock" (2015)

Journal of the American Medical Association (JAMA): "Embryology and Art" (2009)

Kindred Magazine: "Father and Son" (2015)

The Margins: "Death Anniversary," "The First Time I Saw the Sea" (2015)

Massachusetts Review: "Transmigration" (2012)

Measure: "Gather Ye Close-Ups While Ye May," "Nature Show" (2014)

Mezzo Cammin: "Minnesota," "The Patient" (2016)

New Haven Review: "Mitsu" (2016)

The Normal School Online: "Exodus" (2015)

PANK: "Tidal Breathing" (2013)

Portland Review: "The Nymph's Reply to the Shepherd" (2012)

Prelude: "Psych!" (2015)

Raintown Review: "My Imaginary Life as a Narcoleptic" (2014)

The Road Not Taken: "A History of the Cetacean American Diaspora" (2015)

The Southampton Review: "Folk Tale," "Our Metaphors Don't Describe Us; They *Are* Us" (2013)

32 Poems: "A Bruxist Manifesto" (2012)

Two Serious Ladies: "The Faerie Queen Speaks" (2014)

The Village Voice: "Công Binh" (2015)

Water~Stone Review: "Suckling" (2015)

ABOUT THE AUTHOR

Jenna Le is the author of *Six Rivers* (NYQ Books, 2011), which was a Small Press Distribution Poetry Bestseller. *A History of the Cetacean American Diaspora* won Second Place in the 2017 Elgin Awards, voted upon by the international membership of the Science Fiction and Fantasy Poetry Association. Le's poetry, fiction, essays, criticism, translations, and visual art have been published in *AGNI Online, Bellevue Literary Review, Best of the Raintown Review, Denver Quarterly, The Los Angeles Review, Massachusetts Review,* and *West Branch.* Born in Minnesota, Le now lives and works as a physician and educator in New Hampshire.

ABOUT INDOLENT BOOKS

Indolent Books is a small nonprofit poetry press based in Brooklyn. Indolent publishes poetry by underrepresented voices whose work is innovative, provocative, and risky, and that uses all the resources of poetry to address urgent racial, social, and economic justice concerns.

Web: indolentbooks.com
Instagram: @indolent_books
Twitter: @IndolentBooks

www.ingramcontent.com/pod-product-compliance
Lightning Source LLC
Chambersburg PA
CBHW021447080526
44588CB00009B/721